LEGAL INSANITY I

Disorder in the Court

by Steve Rushing

Royal Fireworks Press
Unionville, New York
Toronto, Ontario

Royal Fireworks Press
First Avenue
Unionville, NY 10988
(914) 726-3333
FAX: (914) 726-3824

Royal Fireworks Press
78 Biddeford Avenue
Downsview, Ontario
M3H 1K4 Canada
FAX: (416) 633-3010

ISBN: 0-88092-076-9 Paperback

Printed in the United States of America by the Royal Fireworks Press of Unionville, New York.

FOREWORD

There is a general perception in the United States that attorneys and pond scum are about equally desirable. Those of us who sit on the bench at all levels of the judiciary are not likely to endorse such a dubious proposition. We have heard a great deal of expert testimony from ecologists, marine biologists, and the like as to the desirable traits of pond scum. No such testimony has been offered to us by anyone about attorneys. Most often we hear just the reverse—particularly from the ex-spouses of lawyers.

Nonetheless, one does not have to hang around a courthouse long before one comes to have a sneaking respect for attorneys. It is not the same reverence with which a wetlands advocate approaches pond scum, but respect it is, nevertheless.

The respect I have truly runs counter to the prevailing culture. Normally kind, considerate people laugh uncontrollably about attorneys being buried up to their necks in cement, run over without skid marks, driven off cliffs, or set upon by Doberman Pinchers who attack because they look good on an attorney or hungry Great White Sharks who do not attack only because of professional courtesy.

The members of the Bar I know are not avaricious, pinstriped assassins with the chicanery not seen since W. C. Fields passed from the scene or the killer instincts of Ivan the Terrible. I have never encountered a black robed Tyranasaurus Lex stalking the corridors of Jurisic Court terrorizing defendants and mistreating small children.

Lawyers are survivors. Like the common cockroach, they have been around for a long time and are likely to thrive into the foreseeable future. After years of being the butt of cruel jokes, their skins are at least as tough as the crocodiles, snakes, and other reptiles to which they are constantly compared. And their stomachs are just as tough after years of eating rubber chicken at bar association luncheons.

Like the cockroach, lawyers are prolific. Law schools produce about 40,000 new Juris Doctors each year. Experts estimate that there will be more than a million attorneys in the United States by the new millennium. Given the success of this species, even the most ill-humored attorney should stop splitting hairs, padding fees and waxing eloquent long enough to acquire a sense of humor. And, I don't just mean learning to laugh long and loud at the lamest joke told by any judge.

As for the judiciary, there is a saying that a judge only needs three attributes: grey hair to look distinguished, thick glasses to look learned, and inflamed hemorrhoids to appear concerned. I would submit that a good bladder and a strong sense of humor are important, too!

For me, an escape into the world of legal humor is a pleasant break from the pressures of a job where the eleventh hour seems to come a dozen times a day. Some people play golf or pitch horseshoes. I draw cartoons. I find cartooning helps to maintain perspective, balance, and humility. It also brings pleasure when others enjoy my "legal cartoons" (another lawyerly oxymoron like "speedy trial," "legal action," "attorney ethics," "summary proceeding," or "civil dispute").

Although I lampoon lawyers and make judges into jesters, the cartoons you will encounter here are not really about bashing, smashing, or trashing the legal profession. A long line of cartoonists dating back to the Eighteenth Century and James Gillray have done that. Lawyers have been a tempting target for cartoonists through the centuries because of their close identification with the sub-species politician and other assorted scalawags who happen to have legal training. Other cartoonists such as Honoré Daumier and the cartoonists of *The New Masses* pilloried lawyers for their place in the established order. I am not interested in kicking over the traces of our society. I feel for attorneys much the same affection Bill Maulding had for his famous G.I.'s, Willie and Joe. For attorneys are too frequently on the front lines in our attempts to impose a rule of law on a violent society where the frontier tradition remains alive and the pistol is now as automated as everything else. There are a lot worse things than the clash of legal wills in the court room—and we are altogether too familiar with the worse things.

My cartoons are about learning to appreciate humor where you find it—even in seemingly humorless situations—and about learning to laugh at ourselves. They are my contribution to learning to do what we do best with grace and humor and a sense of irony.

See you in court!

S. O. R.

*To my wife and best friend, Mia, and to our children, Holly,
Whitney, Timothy and Matthew...whose love and laughter
made this book possible."*

Acknowledgements are due to a number of attorneys, judges, litigants and court personnel who unwittingly provided inspiration for this collection of cartoons and whose identity would be indelicate to divulge.

Acknowledgements are also due to certain persons affiliated with the dozens of newspapers and magazines in which I have been fortunate to have my "Legal Insanity" cartoons appear. Among them, without limitation, are Judson H. Orrick and Cheryle M. Dodd, Editor and Managing Editor of the *Florida Bar News/Journal*; Theodore A. Serrill and John J. Tischner, Publisher and Editor of the *Pinellas Review*; Aaron R. Fodiman and Sharon Babbitt, Publisher/Editor and Assistant Editor of the *Tampa Bay Magazine*; Gerald Bennett, Executive Director of American International Syndicate, Inc.; and Floyd E. Egner, III, Publisher of *Tropical Breeze*.

Additionally, I wish to express my appreciation to Dr. T. M. Kemnitz, Chairman of Royal Fireworks Press, for his efforts and expertise in bringing this book into reality.

Most importantly, I thank my judicial assistant, Sherrie Morton, and her husband, Barney Morton, for their behind the scenes work, support and friendship over the years.

STEVE RUSHING

"THE DEFENSE IS READY."

1

"YOU'RE CHARGED WITH POSSESSION OF DRUGS. JUST SIT HERE AND TRY TO LOOK STRAIGHT."

"HOW DID YOUR HEARING GO WITH THE JUDGE?"

LAW SCHOOL 101

THE ART OF CROSS-EXAMINATION

"THIS IS HIGGINS—HE'S OUR CONTRACT
EXCULPATORY CLAUSE SPECIALIST."

7

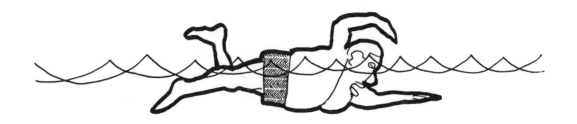

"SO MUCH FOR PROFESSIONAL COURTESY..."

STEVE RUSHING

"I DON'T CARE HOW JUDGE WAPNER RULED ON 'PEOPLE'S COURT'..."

"SOMETIMES I COULD SWEAR THEY SPEED UP..."

"YOUR NAME ISN'T ON OUR LIST, MR. WALLER.
HOWEVER, I MUST INFORM YOU THAT YOU HAVE
30 DAYS IN WHICH TO APPEAL THIS DECISION."

STEVE
PUSHING

"HOW DOES YOUR CLIENT PLEAD TO THIS
CHARGE OF PORNOGRAPHY?"

STEVE RUSHING

"SOMETIMES I FEEL LIKE I'M JUST 'GOING
THROUGH THE MOTIONS.'"

"MUST BE THEIR EXPERT WITNESS ON COMPUTERS."

CROSS EXAMINATION PRACTICE RANGE

CROSS EXAMINATION PRACTICE RANGE

"FEEBERT, THAT'S NOT WHAT WE MEAN BY ATTORNEY-CLIENT PRIVILEGE!"

"AND FURTHERMORE, WE ARE SEEKING
LIQUIDATED DAMAGES."

"BUT I *DID* TELL THE TRUTH...I SAID I'D BE AT COURT FOR THE REST OF THE DAY."

"WORST CASE OF ATTORNEY BURNOUT
I'VE EVER SEEN..."

"DYNAMITE CLOSING, PETE!"

"WHAT KIND OF COURT DID YOU
JUST CALL THIS?"

23

WOULD THE COURT REPORTER PLEASE READ
BACK MY LAST QUESTION?

"HOW DO YOU PLEAD TO THE CHARGES OF
FORGERY AND ESCAPE?"

25

"LET'S SETTLE THIS ONCE AND FOR ALL..JUST WHO IS THE FASTEST GAVEL IN THE CIRCUIT."

"EXCUSE ME, SIR. I'M THE ASSOCIATE AND COULD YOU PLEASE ABBREVIATE THAT 'ASSOC.'?"

"JENKINS, WHEN I SAID 'LET'S PICK SIX!',
I MEANT THE JURY."

"JUDGE, WE'RE PREPARED TO TAKE THIS RULING
TO A HIGHER COURT."

"HE'S OUR IN-HOUSE COUNSEL."

"AT THIS TIME, YOUR HONOR, MY CLIENT WISHES
TO CHANGE HIS PLEA."

"I'M SORRY SIR, BUT HE MUST HAVE STEPPED
AWAY FROM HIS DESK."

"I REALIZE JUSTICE IS BLIND, JUDGE, HOWEVER..."

33

"DECISIONS...DECISIONS..."

"DO YOU HAVE ANY BOOKS ON SPEEDY TRIAL? I
HAVE TO BE IN COURT IN TEN MINUTES."

"SOMETHING'S GONE WRONG WITH OUR
WITNESS HYPNOSIS PROGRAM...HE THINKS
HE'S AN ATTORNEY!"

"I OBJECT TO THIS ATTEMPT TO IMPEACH
THE EYE WITNESS."

"MAYBE IT HAS SOMETHING TO DO WITH THE
SPEEDY TRIAL RULE."

JUDICIAL COLLEGE 101

"HOW'S THE ALTERNATE DISPUTE RESOLUTION
PROGRAM WORKING?"

"HE SAYS HE DOESN'T TRUST HIS CASE
BEFORE A CRIMINAL JUDGE."

"ALRIGHT, WHO STUCK THE BATMAN DECAL ON THE JUDGE'S ROBE?"

"I UNDERSTAND YOU SPECIALIZE IN CONSTITUTIONAL LAW..."

"GET READY, THE DEFENDANT'S TAKING THE STAND NOW..."

45

"I GRABBED THE WRONG ROBE THIS MORNING."

STEVE RUSHING

47

"WON'T YOUR HONOR PLEASE RECONSIDER
DEFENSE COUNSEL'S MOTION FOR
CONTINUANCE?"

"I KNOW YOU'RE AN ATTORNEY, BUT YOU'VE GOT TO STOP READING SO MUCH SMALL PRINT."

"TELL HER I'M AT A BAR FUNCTION."

50

"I REALIZE YOU'RE NEW—BUT NEXT TIME I ASK
YOU TO FILE A SUIT, I MEAN AT THE
COURTHOUSE!"

STEVE RUSHING

"WE FIND THE DEFENDANT GUILTY, BUT WE HAVE A PRESENTATION TO MAKE TO HIS ATTORNEY."

CHIEF JUDGE

STEVE
RUSHING

53

"THIS IS JED, OUR LOCAL COUNSEL."

"I NOW HAND YOU EXHIBIT 'B'
FOR IDENTIFICATION."

"WE'RE STILL DELIBERATING. COULD YOU BRING
SOME MORE SNACKS AND SODAS?"

"TWO GENTLEMEN FROM THE BAR'S ETHICS OFFICE ARE HERE TO SEE YOU, SIR."

"IS THE DEFENDANT READY FOR SENTENCING?"

STEVE RUSHING

"STATUES! I SAID, BRING ME THE STATUTES!"

"I ASSURE YOU THIS GRAND JURY INVESTIGATION
WON'T BE JUST ANOTHER WHITEWASH."

ADMIRALTY LAW

"THE MISTAKES YOU KEEP REFERRING TO AS LITTLE
'OOPSIES,' 'BLOOPERS' AND 'NO-NO'S,'
WE CALL MALPRACTICE..."

"AND NOW, LADIES AND GENTLEMEN OF THE
JURY, I'M GOING TO PROVE THAT MY
CLIENT IS INNOCENT."

"AS A FORMER PROSECUTOR, DO YOU EVER
CATCH YOURSELF WISHING FOR A GOOD OLD
FELONY OR EVEN A LITTLE MISDEMEANOR TO
COME ALONG UP HERE?"

"ANYONE ELSE WANT TO TRY
TO BE FOREPERSON?"

"LOOKS LIKE THE COURT IS LEANING TOWARD
GRANTING OUR MOTION."

"I OBJECT TO THIS EXAMINATION OF THE
WITNESS."

"WE'D LIKE TO FILE A CLASS ACTION SUIT."

"YOUR REQUEST FOR CHANGE OF
VENUE IS DENIED."

"LOOKS LIKE HE'S THROWING HIMSELF ON THE MERCURY OF THE COURT..."

"MAY I REMIND YOU, YOUNG MAN, THAT YOU ARE UNDER OATH HERE TODAY..."

"THIS IS ARNOLD FENSTER, OUR SLIP AND FALL
SPECIALIST—OOPS!"

"PERHAPS THIS WILL REFRESH YOUR RECOLLECTION."

"ISN'T HE TAKING JUDICIAL NOTICE
A LITTLE TOO FAR?"

"I HAVE NO FURTHER QUESTIONS OF THIS WITNESS."

"THIS IS FRANK. HE IS BOARD CERTIFIED IN
MECHANICS LIEN LAW."

"YOU MAY HAVE ANY THREE MOTIONS GRANTED."

"EXCUSE ME, BUT WOULD THE WITNESS MIND
HOLDING THIS FOR MY CROSS EXAMINATION?"

"HAROLD HAS ONE OF THE HEAVIER CASELOADS
IN THE OFFICE."

COURTROOM
ENTRANCE

STEVE RUSHING

"WELL, THEN I GUESS IT'S UNANIMOUS..."

"ON REFLECTION, FRANKIE, MAYBE WE
SHOULDN'T HAVE WAIVED CLOSING ARGUMENT."

STEVE RUSHING
©1993

"HEY! NO JUDGE SHOPPING ALLOWED!"

"MY CLIENT DEMANDS HIS RIGHT
TO A SPEEDY TRIAL."

"I JUST KNEW YOU WEREN'T FEELING YOURSELF...YOU HAVEN'T RAISED AN OBJECTION IN THREE DAYS."

"IS THE DEFENDANT READY FOR SENTENCING?"

ABOUT THE AUTHOR

Having been both a prosecutor and defense attorney before assuming the Bench, Judge Steve Rushing literally "draws" upon his courtroom experience. Besides his nationally syndicated cartoon strip "Legal Insanity" and his previous book "A Funny Thing Happened on the Way to Court," he is a popular humorous speaker at bar and business association gatherings. He resides in Seminole, Florida with his lovely wife, Mia, and their four (but who's counting) young children. Judge Rushing also serves in leadership roles in judicial, legal and community organizations, and is a director and co-founder of Save the Florida Panther, Inc., for which he co-wrote and co-produced the pop record "Save the Panther."

Steve received his Juris Doctorate from Stetson University college of Law in 1975 where he was President of the Student Bar and where he first began drawing "legal" cartoons. He admits that his cartoons have changed some over the years and by sheer coincidence, "the cartoon characters are getting fatter now and they wear glasses, too."

STEVE RUSHING